Start Right Reader

GRADE 2 · BOOK 2

Copyright © by Houghton Mifflin Harcourt Publishing Company

All rights reserved. No part of this work may be reproduced or transmitted in any form or by any means, electronic or mechanical, including photocopying or recording, or by any information storage or retrieval system, without the prior written permission of the copyright owner unless such copying is expressly permitted by federal copyright law. Requests for permission to make copies of any part of the work should be submitted through our Permissions website at https://customercare.hmhco.com/contactus/ Permissions.html or mailed to Houghton Mifflin Harcourt Publishing Company, Attn: Intellectual Property Licensing, 9400 Southpark Center Loop, Orlando, Florida 32819-8647.

Printed in the U.S.A.

ISBN 978-1-328-70203-6

3 4 5 6 7 8 9 10   0928   26 25 24 23 22 21 20 19

4500758494   B C D E F G

If you have received these materials as examination copies free of charge, Houghton Mifflin Harcourt Publishing Company retains title to the materials and they may not be resold. Resale of examination copies is strictly prohibited.

Possession of this publication in print format does not entitle users to convert this publication, or any portion of it, into electronic format.

Contents

Week 1

Week 2

Week 3

MODULE 4

Week 1

Week 2

Week 3

Get Started

In the next stories, King Ben has many fine things, but he is sad. Can his pals Grand Man Stan and Grace make him smile?

Will King Ben ever be glad? Read to find out!

King Ben

Grace

Grand Man Stan

Sad King Ben

by Nico Tate

illustrated by Freya Hartas

King Ben had a big home in a fine land.
He had a nice cape and rings on his hand.
King Ben had a lot, but he did not have a smile.
He just sat, so sad, so sad.

Grace had no rings and no land. She just
had a mop and a smile. "I wish King Ben had
a smile," Grace said.

"King Ben," said Grand Man Stan. "I have just the thing to give you a lift! I have a band."

"Bam!" went the drums. "Pip, pip!" went the pipes.

King Ben held up his hands. "I cannot stand this glad tune!" he said. "The band must stop!"

The band left. King Ben sat in a slump and kept his long, sad face.

"I can sing to you," Grand Man Stan said.

"Fine," King Ben said.

Grand Man Stan did not sing a glad song. He sang a sad song, and it made King Ben sob. Grand Man Stan had to stop.

"King Ben, do you like puppets?" Hope said. She held up a skunk puppet.

"I am a skunk," Hope said. "Hope will name me No Stink!"

Grand Man Stan got up to clap. "Nice joke!" he said. "You are fun, No Stink!"

King Ben did not clap, and he did not smile.

Tom held up a cake he had made. King Ben
ate a bite, but he did not like it.

Grand Man Stan gave up. "King Ben," he
said, "what can we do to help? Give us a hint."

King Ben got up and gave a nod.

"Go on a quest and find a fun thing to make me smile," King Ben said. "If it helps me smile, you get a prize."

Grand Man Stan bit his lip. "I cannot think what to get," he said.

"Send me!" Grace said. "I can go on this quest! I wish to help!"

Poetry Break

Read the words below to a partner. Then read the poem.

wish	sing	long	king	thing
think	hand	land	kept	are

I Am the King

I am a **king**,
a ring on my **hand**.
It's quite a big **thing**,
to rule all the **land**.

I smile and I **sing**
and I go on **long** quests.
I **think** up the rules.
This job is the best!

Would you **wish** to be the king? Why or why not?
Discuss your ideas with your partner.

Blend and Read

1. tennis   tent   hand   bent   band   invent

2. basket   mask   damp   last   trumpet   past

3. ape   bake   bike   mile   smile   base

4. skit   spin   trim   trap   flag   spat

5. clang   lung   prank   mink   flank   stung

6. Did the skunk puppet make King Ben smile?

7. Grand Man Stan sang a sad song.

8. Grace will go on a quest to help King Ben.

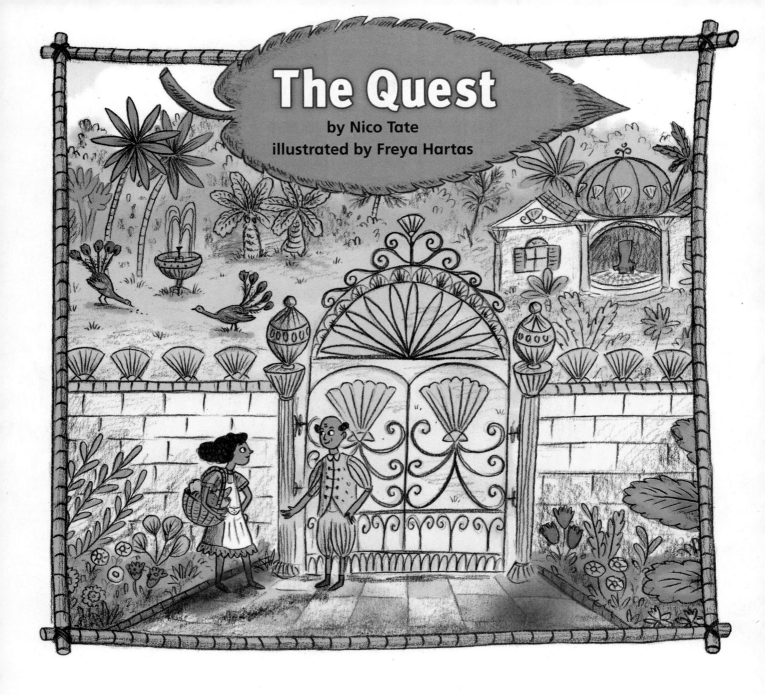

The Quest

by Nico Tate

illustrated by Freya Hartas

Grace and Grand Man Stan went to the gate.

"This task is big," Grand Man Stan said. "King Ben must smile. You must find a fun thing to help him."

"I will," Grace said. "Do not fret, Grand Man. We can make King Ben glad."

Grace went six miles and then made a stop.
"I can use a rest," Grace said. "This pond is nice."
Grace sat next to the pond. A frog swam past. Then, pop! He came on land. Hop! He made a long jump past Grace.
"Nice jump, Frog!" Grace said.

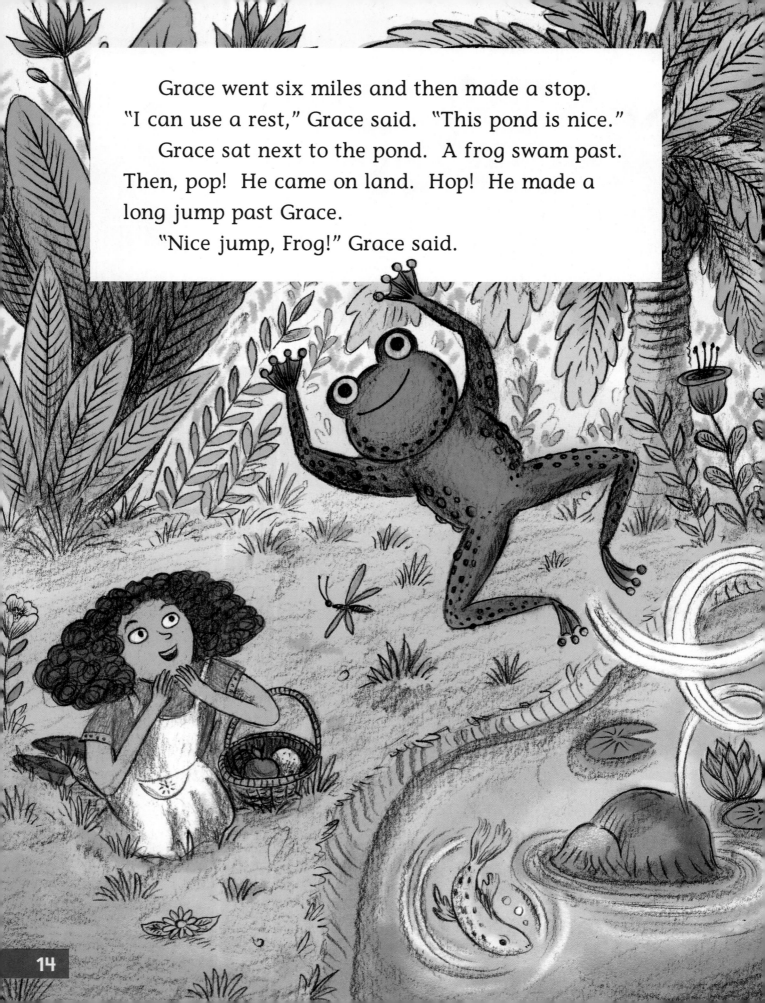

Hop! The frog made a jump at Grace. Plop!
He sat next to her hand.

"Nice frog!" Grace said. "You make me smile.
I think big jumps will make sad King Ben smile.
Can I take you to him?"

"Ribbit!" Frog said.

Grace kept Frog in her basket and went home.

"We have a problem," Grand Man Stan said.
"We held a contest to get King Ben the best gift.
We gave him gumdrops, pretzels, and more, but he
did not smile! You are his last hope."

"I got King Ben a frog," Grace said.

"What!" Grand Man Stan said. "A frog? No!"

Grace went to King Ben.

"I got you a gift," Grace said. Frog sat in her basket. He made a long jump to the king and sat on his trunk.

"Ribbit," Frog said.

Grand Man Stan bit his lip. "A frog cannot sit next to a king!" he said. "King Ben will get mad!"

King Ben did not get mad. He had a big smile!

"I like this frog!" King Ben said. "It can make long jumps. I am not sad. In fact, I am glad!"

Then King Ben said, "We will make Frog a nice, big pond. Grace, what do you wish?"

"No more mops!" Grace sang. "I can tend the frog pond. Frog can give me a hand, and his long jumps will make me smile!"

Retell a Story

Reread both stories. Then choose one story to retell to a partner. Use a chart like this as you plan. Tell what happens first, next, and last.

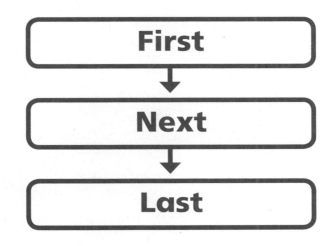

| First |
| Next |
| Last |

Get Started

Roz and Bill are going to the big game. Roz will drive them in her old van.

Will the van get Roz and Bill to the big game on time? Will they have a problem? Read to find out!

The Van

by Bryan Langdo
illustrated by Gediminas Pranckevičius

"It is time to go to the big game!" Bill said. "Can you drive the van, Roz?"

"I can," Roz said. "I did not have time to fix it up, but it will go." The van had dents, rust, and holes.

Bill got his cap. Roz and Bill got in the van. It ran, but it did not run well. Then it got a flat tire!

"Roz, will this van get us to the game on time?" Bill said.

"Do not fret, Bill," Roz said. "It is old, but it still runs fine."

Roz held up a pump.

"You can pump up the tire, Bill," Roz said. "I will fix this and make sure the gas tank is full."

Roz can fix the van and make it run well.
"It is fine, Bill," Roz said. "Hop in."
Putt! Putt! The van ran, but it did not go
fast. It made smoke. Big puffs went up and
made a bad smell.

A car came up at a fast pace. Roz drove off
to the side and let the car pass.

The van crept up the mountain. More smoke went up in puffs.

"Will we make it across the mountain?" Bill said. "Will we miss the game?"

"The van is fine," Roz said. "I think we will be at the game in no time. Trust me."

Then Roz hit a bump. Bang! Hiss! The van came to a sudden stop.

"Roz! Did the van quit?" Bill said. "This is a big problem! We will miss the game."

"No, Bill. It is not a problem," Roz said. "I can fix it."

Roz dug in the van. She got rags and a box. Then she bent down to fix the van.

"It is just a hose," Roz said. "It fell off, but I can fix it. Trust me!"

Roz made the fix, but the van still did not go.
Bill had to push it. The van crept just a bit. Then
it slid across stones and sank down in wet mud.

"No!" Bill said. "This is bad! We will miss the
big game!"

"Yes," Roz said. "This is a big problem."

Story Word Tally

Knowing how to read and write these words can make you a better reader and writer. Make a list of the words.

pull	car	down	full	across
fell	held	spell	push	mountain

1. Look for each word in the story. Make a tally mark each time you find a word.

2. Compare lists with a partner. Which words were used the most? Which words were not used at all?

3. Take turns with your partner. Use each word in a sentence.

Blend and Read

1. buzz   bill   fuzz   bell   hill   hiss

2. miss   missed   tape   tapped   tapping   taping

3. softer   smaller   oldest   coldest   smallest   older

4. blink   clank   clump   stump   blank   stamp

5. chill   shell   chess   prank   champ   dill

6. Will Bill and Roz miss the big game?

7. The van puffed and bumped to a stop.

8. Bill fretted until Roz fixed the hose.

Bill and Roz Get Help

by Bryan Langdo
illustrated by Gediminas Pranckevičius

Roz got in the van and stepped on the gas. The van grunted and puffed smoke. It flung mud on Bill.

"It is just spinning, Roz," Bill said. "It will not go, and it is making a mess."

Roz stopped the van. It huffed, popped, and clanked. Then it went still.

"You must fix it, Roz," Bill yelped. "We will miss the game if the van is trapped in mud!"

"What can I do?" Roz said. "It is not as if I can lift it. We must sit a spell and think."

Just then, Zeke came biking up the hill.

Bill waved to him. "The van is trapped," Bill said. "Can you help us?"

Zeke nodded. "I can help," he said.

Bill and Zeke stepped in the mud.

"Go, Roz, go!" Bill yelled.

The van hissed. Bill and Zeke held on and pushed. The van hummed, but it did not go. Bill slipped and fell down in the mud. The van just kept on sending up smoke and spinning in place.

Zeke and Bill wiped off the mud. Roz shut off the van.

"This is bad!" Bill said. "The van is trapped. We must get help!"

"Bill, stop fretting," Roz said. "I am getting help. It will get fixed."

In a bit, Tess came driving up the hill. Tess had a big rig.

"I can help. It is no problem!" Tess said.
"This rig can use rope to pull the van uphill."

Bill and Zeke got the rope on the van. "Pull, Tess! Push, Zeke!" Bill said. Tess stepped on the gas in the big rig. It dragged the van up to the lane. Mud dripped off its sides.

"The van is a mess," Tess said, "but it is not trapped. You can go home."

"Not yet," Bill said. "Roz and I planned to go to the big game. We will still go if we did not miss it."

"You did not miss it," Tess said. "I am planning to go as well."

"So am I!" Zeke said.

"A full van! We will have a fine time," Roz said.

"At last!" Bill said. "Off we go! No problem!"

Cause and Effect

Reread both stories. Then look at the pictures below. Tell what happens and why. How does one thing lead to another?

1. Draw a picture of what happens next. Write why it happens.

2. Share your work with a partner. Talk about how one thing leads to another.

Get Started

Meet Mr. and Mrs. Mouse. Here are some fun facts about them.

Mr. Mouse	Mrs. Mouse
• bakes cakes	• sees well
• sings songs	• thinks fast
• helps others	• is kind

What will happen to Mr. and Mrs. Mouse?
Who will they meet? Read to find out!

Mice Can Help

by Katherine Rawson
illustrated by Olga Skomorokhova

"We can bake a cake," said Mrs. Mouse.
"We can use these eggs."

"But we do not have milk," Mr. Mouse said.

"Then I shall get milk," Mrs. Mouse said.
"I will go and fetch a bag."

"I will go with you, Bess," said Mr. Mouse,
smiling at his wife.

The mice skipped down the path.

"What is that white thing on the path?"
Mr. Mouse asked. "Is it a rabbit? Is it a hen?"
The mice stopped as Mrs. Mouse gasped.
"That is a big white cat," she yelled. "Run,
Mike! He has spotted us. I think he will get us."

"Run! Run faster, Mike! He will catch us!"
Mrs. Mouse yelled. The mice kept running,
huffing and puffing.

"Jump in this ditch, Bess! Hide!" The mice
dashed off the path and dove in the ditch.

"Hush, Mike," Mrs. Mouse said. "We must
be still. Hush! Do not even blink." The mice
hugged and sat still in the ditch.

Time passed. The mice felt stiff. "I think I am getting a chill, Mike," Mrs. Mouse said.

"Is the white cat still close?" Mr. Mouse asked. "I will go up and see."

"No, Mike! That is not safe," Mrs. Mouse said. "He will spot us. Sit still and hide!"

"But he is just sitting on the path," Mr. Mouse said. "We can help him, Bess."

"Help him? Help a cat?" Mrs. Mouse yelped.
"We do not help cats. Sit still and hide, Mike."

"But this cat is so, so sad," Mr. Mouse said.
"I wish to help him, Bess."

"Well, let me see," Mrs. Mouse said, and up
she went. She faced the white cat.

"Can you help me?" he begged. "I got
jabbed when I went on that path."

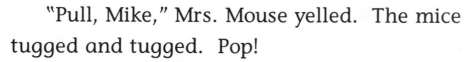

"Pull, Mike," Mrs. Mouse yelled. The mice tugged and tugged. Pop!

"Thanks! Thanks so much!" the cat said.

The cat waved as the mice trotted on the path to the shop. He went on the other path.

"He is such a nice cat," Mrs. Mouse said. "But we must rush, Mike. The shop will be closed if we do not, and we must get that milk!"

Sentence Starters

Read the words below with a partner.

Mr.	Mrs.	mouse	white	while
these	when	even	other	shall

Talk about the story. Use these sentence starters.

1. **Mrs. Mouse** is ____.

2. **Mr. Mouse** is ____.

3. The mice hide **when** ____.

4. **Mr.** and **Mrs. Mouse shall** ____.

5. The **white** cat ____.

Blend and Read

1. chip   which   unlike   ditch   refill   phone

2. dash   rethink   redo   undo   those   unbend

3. mice   pretzel   scale   price   spine   cling

4. lace   helmet   wink   place   sting   plank

5. gash   botch   latch   slash   hitch   graph

6. Mrs. Mouse shall go to the shop.

7. The mice rush to get to the shop.

8. The mice help the white cat.

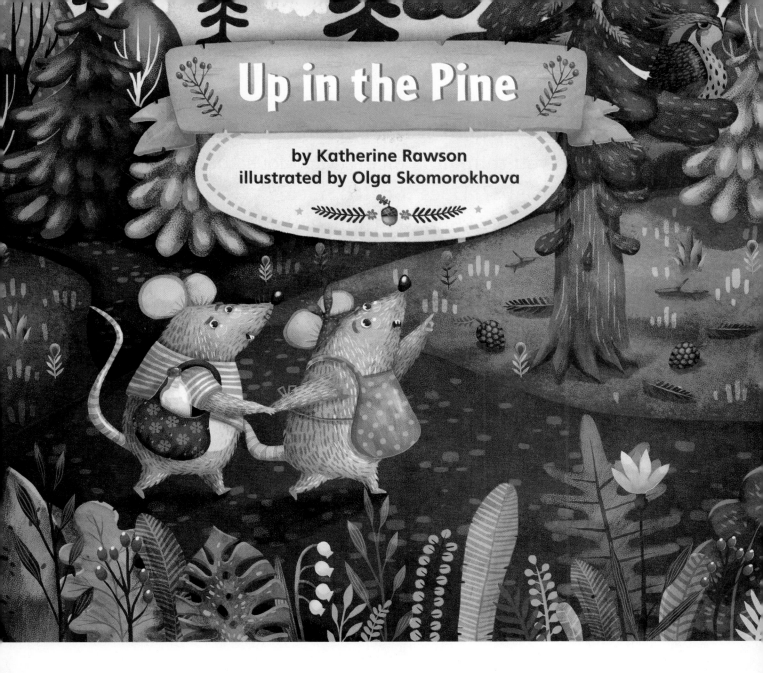

Up in the Pine

by Katherine Rawson
illustrated by Olga Skomorokhova

Mr. and Mrs. Mouse made it to the shop in time. The mice got milk and left the shop.

Mr. Mouse sang a song while the mice skipped home. "Cake is fine. We bake it fast. We bake a cake. It will not last."

Mrs. Mouse stopped skipping. "What is up in that pine?" she asked Mike. "Can you see it, Mike, up at the top?"

"Is it a chipmunk, Bess?" asked Mr. Mouse.

"No, Mike, it is not a chipmunk," she answered. "I think it is a big bird."

"Do you think it is nice?" Mr. Mouse asked. "Can it see us? Does it catch mice?"

"That bird is huge! I think we are unsafe. I cannot be sure," Mrs. Mouse said, "but I think it is time to run."

At that moment, the mice felt a chill.

"It is flying at us!" Mrs. Mouse yelled.
"Run, Mike! Run!"

The big bird swept down and grabbed
Mr. Mouse! "Help! Bess! Let me go! Let me
go!" he yelped.

"Unhand that mouse!" came a yell.

"Yikes!" yipped the big bird as a white cat jumped at it. It dropped Mr. Mouse, flapped its wings, and sped off to the pine.

"It is the white cat!" Mrs. Mouse said. "The white cat saved us! Thanks so much, Cat."

"I am Kid Cat. I am glad I can help," said the cat. "Hop on. I can take you home. Bring that milk you got."

At home, Mr. Mouse undid the bag and got
the milk. He mixed the milk with eggs and
other things that help cakes taste fine. While
the cake baked, Bess, Mike, and Kid Cat
chatted. Bess gave Kid Cat milk in a dish.

"These things take time, Kid," Mrs. Mouse
said. "Sit, relax. Even a big cat must like to
rest. Shall we dine on cake when it is baked?"

"No, thanks, Bess. I must get home to Mrs. Cat and the ten kittens," Kid Cat said. "Can I take a bit home to them?"

"Ten kittens!" Mrs. Mouse said with a big smile. "Take the whole cake home, Kid. I insist. We can redo the baking and replace it. We have got milk and eggs."

"Thanks so much," said Kid as he left.

Story Details

Reread both stories. Then answer the questions.

1. Why do Mr. and Mrs. Mouse go walking on the path?

2. Why do you think Mr. and Mrs. Mouse help the cat?

3. Why do you think the cat helps Mr. and Mrs. Mouse?

4. Do you think the mice and Kid Cat will be pals? Explain.

Talk about your answers with a group.

Get Started

Long ago and far away lived two girls named Bell and Kris. Here are some fun facts about them.

Bell	Kris
• has a grand home	• has a cute little home
• has a grand life	• works for Bell and spends time with her
• is sad	• has ducks, hens, rabbits

What will Bell and Kris do? Can Kris make Bell smile? Read to find out!

→ Bell ←

→ Kris ←

In Times Past: A Grand Life

· by Alan Ruiz ·
illustrated by Josée Masse

Bell has a big, grand home. She has a thick, white rug and a big bed. She has red velvet capes. She has rich frocks and socks made with lace.

Her mother is a grand lady. Bell will be a grand lady when she gets big. Bell has quite a grand life, but she is often a bit sad.

A girl named Kris spends time with Bell.
Helping Bell is her job. She mends velvet capes
and matches lace socks. She makes the big bed
and pins buttons on frocks.

Bell likes to chat with Kris and ask her what
her home is like.

"It is small but cute," Kris tells her. "It has
ducks, hens, and rabbits."

Bell and Kris joke and have fun. When her tasks are done, Kris dashes home. Then Bell is sad. Her mother asks, "Bell, are you sick? You did not have cake."

"I am not sick, but I am sad," Bell tells her. "I do not like this home."

"But it is a big, grand home," her mother answers. "You have such nice things."

"Yes, I do not lack things," Bell states. "I have nice things, and I am filled with thanks. But life can be dull in this grand home."

Bell sips her milk. Then she adds, "I just wish to visit other places. I wish to spend time with ducks and hens. I wish to hug cute little rabbits."

"I will buy you ducks, hens, and cute little rabbits then," her mother states.

"No, thank you," Bell answers. She wipes her face with a soft cloth napkin. Then she asks, "Can I go with Kris to see her home?"

"Yes! You can visit Kris," her mother answers. She kisses Bell and adds, "Ask Kris the next time you see her."

Bell sees Kris at sunrise. She jumps up and down and asks, "Can I visit you at home? I asked Mother. She said it is fine!"

Kris smiles and yells, "Yes! I am so glad. We will have such fun!"

Bell and Kris dig in a trunk. Bell gets an old frock and cape and packs a basket. She and Kris wave and run off down the path.

Secret Word Game

 Play with a partner.
Use a timer. Take turns.

ask	asked	buy	comb	girl
grand	lady	mother	number	often

1. Think of a word in the box.

2. Set the timer.

3. Tell a clue about the word.

4. Your partner tries to guess the secret word.

5. Continue until your partner guesses or time runs out.

The first to guess five secret words wins!

Blend and Read

1. black   block   tack   knock   knit   frock

2. check   peck   stack   wreck   stuck   wrap

3. milk   bend   bell   unbend   hill   help

4. ten   rock   drop   tennis   rocket   gumdrop

5. writer   cracker   quicker   sticker   wrapper

6. Bell got knots in her hair. Kris combed it.

7. Mother asked Bell if she felt sick.

8. Bell wished to visit Kris.

At Home with Kris
· by Alan Ruiz ·
illustrated by Josée Masse

Bell and Kris run up the hill. At the top, Bell spots a sign with the number six on it.

"This is it!" Kris tells Bell.

Kris and Bell dash down the path. The little home is wrapped in pink roses and vines.

"What a nice home!" Bell sings.

Kris grins. "Come on in, Bell!"

"Bell, this is Nick." Kris pats Nick on his back. "Nick is ten."

Kris takes Nick and Bell to a pen.

Bell smiles at the black and white hens in the pen. Little chicks peck at bugs. Ducks quack and rabbits hop. Bell picks up a cute little rabbit and hugs it.

"That rabbit is named Patches," Kris tells her.

Bell spends time helping Kris and Nick. Kris knits, so Bell knits. Nick chops logs, so Bell chops logs. Kris and Nick find eggs in nests, so Bell finds eggs in nests. Kris and Nick get milk, so Bell gets milk.

"I like seeing what it is like to have jobs," Bell states.

Then the girls have fun at the swing.

"Hop on. I will push you," Kris tells Bell.

The sun shines on Bell and Kris. Wrens sing. Bees buzz in the roses. Bell smiles. She is so glad to be at home with Kris. She is so glad to have Kris and Nick as pals.

"Yum!" Nick yells. "Mother made us muffins!"

The kids rush back inside and get a snack.

At sunset, a man comes to fetch Bell and bring her home. Bell tells Kris, "I had so much fun. I have a gift to give you."

Bell picks up her basket. In it sits a fine comb. "This comb is like mine," she notes.

"It is so grand! I will use it often. Thank you!" Kris tells her.

Kris winks at Nick. It is time to give Bell a gift.

Back at home, Bell and Patches are snug in bed. Bell wraps herself in a thick red robe and sets a pad on her lap. She picks up a pencil and taps it on the pad. Then she smiles.

"This tale will tell what happened when I went to visit Kris at her home," she writes. "I am so glad I went. What a grand time I had!"

Compare and Contrast

Reread both stories. Use details from your reading to answer the questions.

1. How are Bell and Kris the same? How are they different?

2. How are their homes alike? How are they different?

3. How does Bell feel in **In Times Past: A Grand Life?** Why?

4. How does she feel in **At Home with Kris?** Why?

Turn and Talk

Share your answers with a partner.

Get Started

Meet Tess and Jay! They are going sailing. Will Tess and Jay have fun? Is it a good plan to sail on a gray day? Read to find out!

Tess

Jay

Tess and Jay Set Sail

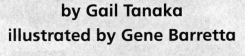

by Gail Tanaka

illustrated by Gene Barretta

"I am going sailing," Tess said. "Will you come with me?"

"Which way will you go?" Jay asked.

"I am going five miles west," Tess said. "I am planning to find a nice little spot to paint and have a picnic. I hope you will come. What do you say, Jay?"

"I think I will stay home," Jay said. "Five
miles is quite a way to go, and it is not a nice
day to sail. This website says it may rain."

"This ship is in great shape," Tess said. "We
will stay safe in it. And see this picnic basket?
It is filled with snacks. I even baked a cake."

"Cake!" Jay licked his lips and hopped in.

Tess and Jay set sail in the bay. Waves made the ship rock. It bobbed up and down. It tilted and swayed. Jay felt an odd knot inside him. He felt a bit sick.

A big wave crashed. Jay grabbed the sides and held on.

"Tess, this trip is making me ill," Jay said. "I am afraid I may faint."

"Stay strong, Jay," Tess said. "Help me with this rope."

Jay tugged on the rope with Tess. The sail flapped, and the ship went left. It passed a rock with ducks on it.

Jay felt a drop hit his tail. Another drop hit his nose. Then the rain came down fast.

"Tess, I am getting really wet," Jay said.

Crack! Bam! A flash lit up the gray day. Rain came down faster. The ship bucked and swayed as waves swept across the deck. Rain filled the ship. It became a bathtub!

Jay gasped as the ship filled up to his waist.

"Quick, Jay!" Tess yelled. "Grab that pail! We must drain the ship!"

Jay swung the pail as Tess sailed the ship.

"I see land," Tess said. "We must try to make it. Do not stop bailing!"

Just then, the ship ran into a rock. Crunch!

"Yikes! That rock made a great big hole in the ship!" Tess yelled. "We are sinking!"

"This is a bad day," Jay sobbed. "I wish I had stayed at home!"

Use That Word

Take turns. Play with a friend until you use all the words.

afraid	always	another	great	passed
says	stay	really	try	which

1. Pick a word and read it.

2. Your friend uses the word in a sentence.

3. Then your friend picks a word and reads it.

4. You use your friend's word in a sentence.

Blend and Read

1. grade   grain   paint   repaint   rail   railway

2. play   replay   lake   label   raid   raided

3. ship   shell   itch   with   thing   which

4. kick   kicking   wake   waking   spill   spilled

5. plainly   mainly   faintly   brainy   playful

6. Tess says she will sail to a fine place.

7. Is Jay always afraid to sail on a gray day?

8. Tess passed the bailing pail to Jay.

A Wrecked Ship!

by Gail Tanaka

illustrated by Gene Barretta

"The ship has sunk, Jay," Tess said.

Jay and Tess stepped off the ship and jumped onto the sand.

"I hate to complain," Jay said, "but this day has sunk, just like the ship."

"I am not upset," Tess said. "We can just take that lane and hike home. It is less than a mile."

It got colder. Little ice bits mixed with the rain.

"It is hailing," Jay said. "This is really bad!"

Hail pelted Tess and Jay. Big hailstones snapped twigs.

"It is as if rocks are being flung at us," Jay wailed to Tess.

"Behave, Jay," said Tess. "Help me drag the ship onto the sand. We can escape the hail."

Tess and Jay flipped the ship and hid inside.
"This is safe," Tess said.

"It is like a snug little hut," Jay said. "We can stay in it until the hail stops."

"The picnic basket got wet," Tess said, a bit dismayed. "The cake may be mush, but I will give wet cake a try. It will be great to have a snack."

"Yum," Jay said as he lifted the picnic basket lid. Then he gasped.

"The cake is missing, Tess!" Jay said. "It must have drifted off with the waves. We just have six wet bagels left. Yuck."

Jay and Tess ate wet bagels. Hail still fell. It banged on the ship.

"This is like sitting in a big drum," Jay said.

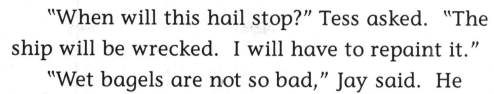

"When will this hail stop?" Tess asked. "The ship will be wrecked. I will have to repaint it."

"Wet bagels are not so bad," Jay said. He picked up pink shells and blue shells. Then he grinned and made lines in the sand.

"We can play a game, Tess!" he said.

Tess and Jay played and replayed the game.

"Well, Jay," Tess said. "Things did not go as planned, but this is still a great day."

Jay gave his pal a pat on the back.

"I always have fun with you, Tess. I am glad I did not stay home."

"We will fix the ship," Tess said. "We will bake another cake and sail another day!"

Think-Write-Pair-Share

Reread both stories. Think and then write answers to these questions.

1. Why does Jay plan to stay home? Why does he change his mind and go with Tess?

2. What are two problems that Jay and Tess have on their trip? How do they resolve the problems?

3. Why do Tess and Jay think they had a great day?

Share your work with a partner and then in a group.

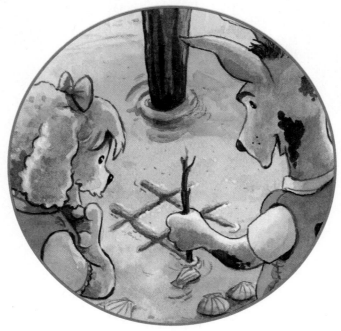

Get Started

What do you know about horses? What must you do to take care of a horse? What are the rules for riding a horse?

What jobs can horses do? Read to find out!

Queen

by Sara Ford
illustrated by Kristi Valiant

I have a horse. Her name is Queen. She is bay, which means she is a bit red with a black mane and tail. She has legs with white socks!

Queen runs to greet me when she sees me. She pushes me with her nose. I feel her breath puffing at me. That is the way she says, "Please feed me treats!"

I pat her head and neck. "Hi, baby!" I say.

It is a big job to keep a horse. I have quite a task list each day!

Queen grazes on grass, and she is fed grain twice a day. I make sure she gets her meals on time. I keep her hay net full so she can eat hay when she feels like it.

I make sure her pails are clean and filled up so she can drink.

Queen sleeps in her pen, which I need to keep clean. I use a rake to pick things up and fill the pen with fresh bedding. Queen can sleep standing up, but she likes to sleep on the ground as well.

The old bedding is a mess. I take it off to dump it on a big heap. I need to get her clean, fresh bedding.

Each day I brush Queen. This gets dust and grime off her neck, sides, back, and legs. She gets nice and sleek, and she gleams when I am done. I can see that she is in fine shape.

Queen gets knots in her mane and tail, so I must comb them. I clean her feet with a small pick. I make sure that no little stones remain stuck in her feet.

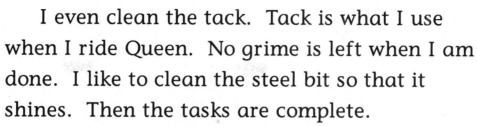

I even clean the tack. Tack is what I use when I ride Queen. No grime is left when I am done. I like to clean the steel bit so that it shines. Then the tasks are complete.

It is time to ride at last. I tack up Queen. (That means getting the tack on her.) I check the tack to make sure it fits well. I cannot let it rub Queen. That can make her feel pain.

Then I get up on Queen. I always get up on her left side. That is a rule when you ride horses.

We leave home and head down the lane. Then we trot past an old pine tree. Queen speeds up as we step onto a path. Off we go! We will have a fun day riding in the green hills.

Story Break

Read this story with a partner.

1. Mom, have you **seen Queen?**

2. I **need** to **clean** her feet.

3. I need to brush her and make her **feel** sleek.

4. I see **horse** prints on the **ground.**

5. Did Queen **leave?**

6. Wait! I see her tail in the **trees.**

7. Queen, **please** stop playing hide-and-seek!

Role-play with a partner. Take turns reading the lines. Work together to brush and clean Queen.

Blend and Read

1. cream   freeze   pleases   sneeze   squeal   secret

2. head   green   sweat   greet   repeat   instead

3. bump   best   button   tested   stump   chest

4. bay   braid   staying   painting   brain   unmade

5. cheer   creamy   reason   neater   pleasant

6. Please feed Queen and clean her pen.

7. Queen likes sleeping on fresh bedding.

8. Queen and I leave and head up the path.

Horses with Jobs

by Sara Ford

© Mavrick/Shutterstock

Have you seen horses do jobs? Horses can help us. Horses can go fast and take us to places we cannot reach with ease. Horses can help us do big tasks.

This horse helps on a ranch. He helps men tend the sheep that graze on hills. He helps bring the sheep back home.

Horses are strong, and we can use them to pull things. This horse pulls a wagon. A tug on the lines tells the horse which way to go.

This horse is such a big help. He walks between the wagon poles, doing his job. Then, at a nice shade tree, he will rest and eat grain.

© Diane Randell / Alamy

This horse helps keep us safe. He is big, so the man on his back can see way down the street! When help is needed, a horse like this can run fast and take the man to those places.

This brave horse is trained not to be afraid when cars and trucks beep and honk. He will not stand up on his back legs and try to leave. Instead, he will stand still and let the man help.

© wizdata/Shutterstock

This horse is an athlete. He is trained to compete! The girl on his back is an athlete as well. The horse and girl make a fine team.

In this contest, the horse runs and leaps. He dashes at jumps that are made using poles. He must run fast and leap with grace. He must leap so that he does not knock the poles to the ground. The best teams will win prizes.

© Marcel Jancovic/Shutterstock

This horse has a job that is fun. Little kids get on her back, and she takes them on rides up and down paths. Then she trots with them in a ring. She is teaching them to ride!

The kids like these riding lessons. Each kid has a helmet. A helmet helps keep you safe when you ride a horse.

© Marcel Jancovic/Shutterstock

Does this horse have a job? No. This horse lives free. He has no shed to stay in when the days are cold and wet, but he is fine with that!

He uses his day as he pleases. He runs with other horses. He can eat grass and sleep when he likes. He can buck and squeal and kick up his heels. A job? No, thanks! Not when he can race with his pals instead!

© Getty Images

Idea Web

Reread both texts. Make an idea web to share what you learned about horses.

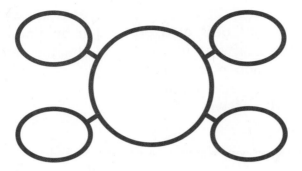

1. Write the word **horses** in the big circle.

2. Write details about horses in the small ovals.

3. Use your web to talk about horses with some partners.

© Getty Images

WORD LISTS

MODULE 3 ■ WEEK 1

BOOK 1 **Sad King Ben** p. 5

■ Decodable Words

TARGET SKILL: *Final Blends*

and*, band, grand*, held*, help*, hint, just*, left*, lift, must*, quest, rings, sang, send, skunk, slump, song, stand, stink, went*

PREVIOUSLY TAUGHT SKILLS

am*, ate*, bam, Ben, big*, bit, bite, but*, cake, can*, cannot*, cape, clap, did*, drums, face, fine, fun*, gave*, get*, glad, go*, got*, Grace, had*, he*, his*, home*, hope, I*, if*, in*, it*, joke, like*, lip, lot*, made*, make*, man*, me*, mop, name*, nice, no*, nod, not*, on*, pip, pipes, prize, puppet, puppets, sad, sat*, smile, so*, sob, Stan, stop*, Tom, tune, up*, us*, we*, will*

■ High-Frequency Words

NEW

are, hand, hands, kept, king, land, long, sing, thing, think, wish

PREVIOUSLY TAUGHT

a, do, find, give, have, said, she, the, this, to, what, you

BOOK 2 **The Quest** p. 13

■ Decodable Words

TARGET SKILLS: *Final Blends; Closed Syllables*

am*, and*, at*, basket, Ben, best*, big*, bit, but*, can*, cannot*, contest, did*, fact, fret, frog, fun, get*, gift, glad, got*, grand*, gumdrops, had*, held*, help*, him*, his*, hop, in*, is*, it*, jump*, jumps*, last, lip, mad, man*, mops, must*, next*, not*, on*, past, plop, pond, pop, pretzels, problem, quest, rest, ribbit, sad, sat*, sang, sit*, six, Stan, stop*, swam, task, tend, trunk, went*

PREVIOUSLY TAUGHT SKILLS

came*, gate, gave*, Grace, he*, home*, hope, I*, like*, made*, make*, me*, miles, nice, no*, smile, take*, use*, we*

■ High-Frequency Words

NEW

are, hand, kept, king, land, long, thing, think, wish

PREVIOUSLY TAUGHT

a, do, find, give, have, her, more, said, the, then, this, to, what, will, you

BOOK 1 **The Van** p. 21

■ Decodable Words

TARGET SKILL: *Double Final Consonants*

Bill, hiss, miss*, off*, pass*, puffs, putt, smell, still*, well*, will*

PREVIOUSLY TAUGHT SKILLS

and*, at*, bad*, bang, be*, bent, big*, bit, box, bump, but*, came*, can*, cap, crept, dents, did*, drive, drove, dug, fast*, fine, fix, flat, fret, game, gas, get*, go*, got*, had*, his*, hit*, holes, hop, hose, I*, in*, is*, it*, just*, let*, made*, make*, me*, mud, no*, not*, on*, pace, problem, pump, quit, rags, ran*, Roz, run*, runs*, rust, sank, side*, slid, smoke, stones, stop*, sudden, tank, time*, tire, trust, up*, us*, van, we*, went*, wet, yes*

■ High-Frequency Words

NEW

across, car, down, fell, full, held, mountain, push

PREVIOUSLY TAUGHT

a, do, have, more, old, said, she, sure, the, then, think, this, to, you

BOOK 2 **Bill and Roz Get Help** p. 29

■ Decodable Words

TARGET SKILLS: *Double Final Consonants; Inflections*

biking, Bill, clanked, dragged, dripped, driving, fixed, fretting, getting*, grunted, hill, hissed, huffed, hummed, making*, mess, miss*, nodded, off*, planned*, planning*, popped, puffed, sending, sides*, slipped, spinning, stepped, still*, stopped*, Tess, trapped, uphill, waved, well*, will*, wiped, yelled, yelped

PREVIOUSLY TAUGHT SKILLS

am*, and*, as*, at*, bad*, big*, bit, but*, came*, can*, did*, fine, fix, flung, game, gas, get*, go*, got*, had*, he*, help*, him*, home*, I*, if*, in*, is*, it*, its*, just*, kept*, lane, last, lift, mud, must*, no*, not*, on*, place, problem, rig, rope, Roz, shut, sit*, smoke, so*, stop*, time*, up*, us*, use*, van, we*, went*, yet*, Zeke

■ High-Frequency Words

NEW

down, fell, full, held, pull, push, pushed, spell

PREVIOUSLY TAUGHT

a, do, have, said, the, then, think, this, to, what, you

BOOK 1 **Mice Can Help** p. 37

■ Decodable Words

TARGET SKILL: *Consonant Digraphs*

catch, chill, dashed, ditch, fetch, hush, much*, path, rush, shop*, such*, she*, thanks*, that*, then*, thing*, think*, this*, wish*, with*

PREVIOUSLY TAUGHT SKILLS

am*, and*, as*, asked*, at*, bag, bake, be*, begged, Bess, big*, blink, but*, cake, can*, cat, cats, close*, closed*, dove, eggs, faced, faster, felt*, gasped, get*, getting*, go*, got*, has*, he*, help*, hen, hide, him*, his*, huffing, hugged, I*, if*, in*, is*, it*, jabbed, jump*, just*, kept*, let*, me*, mice, Mike, milk, must*, nice, no*, not*, off*, on*, passed*, pop, puffing, rabbit, run*, running*, sad, safe, sat*, sit*, sitting*, skipped, smiling, so*, spot, spotted, stiff, still*, stopped*, time*, trotted, tugged, up*, us*, use*, waved, we*, well*, went*, wife, will*, yelled, yelped

■ High-Frequency Words
NEW

even, mouse, Mr., Mrs., other, shall, these, when, white

PREVIOUSLY TAUGHT

a, do, down, have, pull, said, see, the, to, what, you

BOOK 2 **Up in the Pine** p. 45

■ Decodable Words

TARGET SKILLS: *Consonant Digraphs; Prefixes* un-, re-

catch, chatted, chill, chipmunk, dish, much*, redo, relax, replace, she*, shop*, thanks*, that*, them*, things*, think*, undid, unhand, unsafe, whole, with*

PREVIOUSLY TAUGHT SKILLS

am*, and*, as*, asked*, at*, bag, bake, baked, baking, be*, Bess, big*, bit, bring*, but*, cake, cakes, came*, can*, cannot*, cat, dine, dropped, eggs, fast*, felt*, fine, flapped, gave*, get*, glad, go*, got*, grabbed, he*, help*, home*, hop, huge, I*, in*, insist, is*, it*, its*, jumped*, kid, kittens, last, left*, let*, like*, made*, me*, mice, Mike, milk, mixed, moment, must*, nice, no*, not*, off*, on*, pine, rest, run*, sang, saved, sit*, skipped, skipping, smile, so*, song, sped, stopped*, swept, take*, taste, ten, time*, top, up*, us*, we*, will*, wings, yell, yelled, yelped, yikes, yipped

■ High-Frequency Words
NEW

even, mouse, Mr., Mrs., other, shall, these, when, while, white

PREVIOUSLY TAUGHT

a, answered, are, bird, do, does, down, flying, have, said, see, sure, the, to, what, you

* = High-Frequency Word

BOOK 1 **In Times Past: A Grand Life** p. 53

■ Decodable Words
TARGET SKILL: *Consonants k, ck*
basket, cake, ducks, frock, frocks, joke, kisses, Kris, lack, like*, likes*, makes*, milk, napkin, packs, sick, socks, tasks, thank*, thanks*, thick, trunk

PREVIOUSLY TAUGHT SKILLS
adds, am*, an*, and*, at*, be*, bed, bell, big*, bit, but*, buttons, can*, cape, capes, chat, cloth, cute, dashes, did*, dig, dull, face, filled, fine, fun*, gets*, glad, go*, has*, helping*, hens, home*, hug, I*, in*, is*, it*, job, jumps*, just*, lace, life*, made*, matches, mends, named*, next*, nice, no*, not*, off*, on*, past, path, pins, places*, quite, rabbits, red*, rich, rug, run*, sad, she*, sips, smiles, so*, soft, spend, spends, states*, such*, sunrise, tells*, then*, things*, this*, time*, times*, up*, velvet, visit, wave, we*, when*, white*, will*, wipes, wish*, with*, yells, yes*

■ High-Frequency Words
NEW
ask, asked, asks, buy, girl, grand, lady, mother, often

PREVIOUSLY TAUGHT
a, answers, are, do, done, down, have, her, little, old, other, said, see, sees, small, the, to, what, you

BOOK 2 **At Home with Kris** p. 61

■ Decodable Words
TARGET SKILLS: *Consonants k, ck; Silent Letters (kn, wr, gn, mb)*
back*, basket, black, chicks, ducks, kids, knits, Kris, like*, milk, Nick, peck, picks*, pink, quack, sign, snack, takes*, thank*, thick, winks, wrapped, wraps, wrens, writes*

PREVIOUSLY TAUGHT SKILLS
am*, and*, as*, at*, be*, bed, bees, bell, bring*, bugs, buzz, chops, cute, dash, eggs, fetch, fine, fun*, get*, gets*, gift, glad, grins, had*, happened*, helping*, hens, hill, his*, home*, hop, hugs, I*, in*, inside*, is*, it*, jobs, lap, logs, made*, man*, mine, much*, muffins, named*, nests, nice, notes, on*, pad, pals, patches, path, pats, pen, pencil, rabbit, rabbits, red*, robe, roses, run*, rush, sets*, she*, shines, sing*, sings*, sits*, six, smiles, snug, so*, spends, spots, states*, sun, sunset, swing, tale, taps, tell*, tells*, ten, that*, then*, this*, time*, top, up*, us*, use*, vines, visit, went*, when*, white*, will*, with*, yells, yum

■ High-Frequency Words
NEW
comb, girls, grand, mother, number, often

PREVIOUSLY TAUGHT
a, are, come, comes, down, find, finds, give, have, her, herself, little, push, seeing, the, to, what, you

= High-Frequency Word

BOOK 1 **Tess and Jay Set Sail** p. 69

■ Decodable Words

TARGET SKILL: *Long a Patterns*

bailing, baked, bay, became, cake, came*, day*, drain, faint, gray, Jay, made*, make*, making*, may*, pail, paint, rain*, safe, sail, sailed, sailing, say*, shape, swayed, tail, waist, wave, waves, way*

PREVIOUSLY TAUGHT SKILLS

am*, an*, and*, as*, asked*, at*, bad*, bam, basket, bathtub, big*, bit, bobbed, bucked, crack, crashed, crunch, deck, drop, ducks, even*, fast*, faster, felt*, filled, five, flapped, flash, gasped, getting*, go*, going*, grab, grabbed, had*, he*, held*, help*, him*, his*, hit, hole, home*, hope, hopped, I*, ill, in*, inside*, is*, it*, just*, knot, land*, left*, licked, lips, lit, me*, miles, must*, nice, nose, not*, odd, on*, picnic, planning, quick, quite, ran*, rock*, rope, set*, ship, sick, sides*, sinking, snacks, sobbed, spot, stop*, strong, swept, swung, Tess, that*, then*, think*, this*, tilted, trip, tugged, up*, we*, website, went*, west, wet, will*, wish*, with*, yelled, yikes

■ High-Frequency Words

NEW

afraid, another, great, passed, really, says, stay, stayed, try, which

PREVIOUSLY TAUGHT

a, across, are, come, do, down, find, have, into, little, said, see, the, to, what, you

BOOK 2 **A Wrecked Ship!** p. 77

■ Decodable Words

TARGET SKILLS: : *Long a Patterns; Multisyllabic Words: Long a*

ate*, bagels, bake, behave, cake, complain, day*, dismayed, escape, gave*, game, hail, hailing, hailstones, hate, Jay, lane, made*, may*, play*, played*, rain*, repaint, replayed, safe, sail, take*, wailed, waves

PREVIOUSLY TAUGHT SKILLS

am*, and*, as, asked*, at*, back*, bad*, banged, basket, be*, being*, big*, bit, bits, but*, can*, did*, drag, drifted, drum, fell*, fix, flipped, flung, fun*, gasped, glad, go*, got*, grinned, has*, he*, help*, hid, hike, his*, home*, hut, I*, ice, if*, in*, inside*, is*, it*, jumped*, just*, left*, less, lid, lifted, like*, lines*, me*, mile, missing*, mixed, mush, must*, not*, off*, on*, onto, pal, pat, pelted, picked*, picnic, pink, planned, rocks, sand, shells, ship, sitting*, six, snack, snapped, snug, so*, stepped, still*, stop*, stops*, sunk, Tess, than*, that*, then*, things*, this*, twigs, until*, upset, up*, us*, we*, well*, wet, when*, will*, with*, wrecked, yuck, yum

■ High-Frequency Words

NEW

always, another, great, really, stay, try

PREVIOUSLY TAUGHT

a, are, blue, colder, give, have, little, said, the, to, you

BOOK 1 **Queen** p. 85

■ Decodable Words

TARGET SKILL: *Long* e, *Short* e *Patterns*

baby*, breath, complete*, each*, eat*, even*, feed, feet, gleams, green*, greet, head*, heap, keep*, me*, meals, means, see*, sees*, sleek, sleep*, sleeps*, speeds, steel, treats, we*

PREVIOUSLY TAUGHT SKILLS

am*, an*, and*, as*, at*, back*, bay, bedding, big*, bit, black, brush, but*, can*, cannot*, check, comb, day*, drink, dump, dust, fed, fill, filled, fine, fits, fresh, fun*, get*, gets*, getting*, go*, grain, grass, grazes, grime, has*, hay, hi, hills, home*, I*, in*, is*, it*, job, knots, lane, last, left*, legs, let*, like*, likes*, list, make*, mane, mess, must*, name*, neck, net, nice, no*, nose, off*, on*, onto, pails, pain, past, pat, path, pen, pick*, pine, puffing, quite, rake, red*, remain, ride*, riding*, rub, rule, runs*, say*, shape, she*, shines, side*, sides*, so*, socks, standing, step, stones, stuck, tack, tail, take*, task, tasks, that*, them*, then*, things*, this*, time*, trot, twice, up*, use*, way*, well*, when*, which*, white*, will*, with*

■ High-Frequency Words

NEW

clean, feel, feels, ground, horse, horses, leave, need, please, queen, tree

PREVIOUSLY TAUGHT

a, always, are, done, down, full, have, her, little, old, pushes, says, small, sure, the, to, what, you

---

BOOK 2 **Horses with Jobs** p. 93

■ Decodable Words

TARGET SKILLS: *Long* e, *Short* e *Patterns; Multisyllabic Words:*
Long, Short e

athlete, be*, beep, between, compete, dashes, each*, ease, eat*, free, he*, heels, instead, keep*, leap, leaps, needed*, reach*, see*, she*, sheep, sleep*, squeal, street*, teaching, team, teams, these*, we*

PREVIOUSLY TAUGHT SKILLS

an*, and*, as*, at*, back*, best*, big*, brave, bring*, buck, but*, can*, cannot*, contest, day*, days*, fast*, fine, fun*, get*, go*, grace, grain, grass, graze, has*, helmet, help*, helps*, hills, his*, home*, honk, in*, is*, job, jobs, jumps*, kick, kid, kids, knock, legs, lessons, let*, like*, likes*, lines*, made*, make*, man*, men*, must*, nice, no*, not*, on*, pals, paths, places*, poles, prizes, race, ranch, rest, ride*, rides*, riding*, ring, run*, runs*, safe, shade, shed, so*, stand, stay*, still*, strong, such*, take*, takes*, tasks, tells*, tend, thanks*, that*, them*, then*, things*, this*, those*, trained, trots, trucks, tug, up*, us*, use*, uses*, using*, wagon, way*, well*, wet, when*, which*, will*, win, with*

■ High-Frequency Words

NEW

ground, horse, horses, leave, pleases, seen, tree

PREVIOUSLY TAUGHT

a, afraid, are, cars, cold, do, does, doing, down, girl, have, her, little, lives, other, pull, pulls, the, to, try, walks, you